Luther Library
Midland University
900 N. Clarkson St.
Fremont, NE 68025

W9-BWJ-751

Children of the Dust Bowl

The True Story
of the School at Weedpatch Camp

Children of the Dust Bowl

The True Story
of the School at Weedpatch Camp

JERRY STANLEY

ILLUSTRATED WITH PHOTOGRAPHS

CROWN PUBLISHERS, INC. · New York

Juv
371.9675
St25c

LUTHER LIBRARY
MIDLAND COLLEGE
FREMONT, NE 68025

Copyright © 1992 by Jerry Stanley

All rights reserved. No part of this book may be reproduced or transmitted in any form or by any means, electronic or mechanical, including photocopying, recording, or by any information storage and retrieval system, without permission in writing from the publisher.

Published by Crown Publishers, Inc., a Random House company, 225 Park Avenue South, New York, New York 10003

CROWN is a trademark of Crown Publishers, Inc. Manufactured in the United States of America

Maps by Susan Johnston Carlson

Library of Congress Cataloging-in-Publication Data

Stanley, Jerry, 1941–
Children of the Dust Bowl : the true story of the school at Weedpatch Camp / Jerry Stanley.
— 1st ed.
    p.   cm.
Includes bibliographical references and index.
Summary: Describes the plight of the migrant workers who traveled from the Dust Bowl to California during the Depression and were forced to live in a federal labor camp and discusses the school that was built for their children.
1. Children of migrant workers—Education—California—Arvin—History—20th century—Juvenile literature.   2. Droughts—Southwestern States—History—20th century—Juvenile literature.   3. Depressions—1929—Great Plains—Juvenile literature.   4. Depressions—1929—Southwestern States—Juvenile literature.
[1. Migrant labor—California.   2. Depressions—1929.]   I. Title.
LC5152.C2S73   1992
371.96′75′0979488—dc20   92-393
ISBN 0-517-58781-5 (trade)
0-517-58782-3 (lib. bdg.)
10 9 8 7 6 5 4 3 2 1   First Edition

Picture credits appear on pages 79-80.

18954

To Leo Hart, the teachers, and the children

Contents

Author's Note

The term "Okie" is used in this book as the Okies used it in the 1930s and still do today. Although used by others as a term of abuse, to the Okies themselves it meant pride, courage, and a determination to accept hardship without showing weakness.

INTRODUCTION
Mr. Steinbeck's Book

In 1936 a newspaper reporter named John Steinbeck became interested in a group of people in California who called themselves "Okies." The Okies had once been poor dirt farmers in Oklahoma, Texas, Arkansas, and Missouri. But the Great Depression of the 1930s and a drought in the Great Plains states forced the Okies to leave their homes and head for California, where they had heard pickers were needed to work in the cotton fields and orchards of the San Joaquin Valley.

When they arrived in California, the migrants discovered that few jobs were available. They also discovered that many Californians didn't want Okies in the state. The Okies were poor and uneducated, and their baggy pants, ragged dresses, and desperate-looking faces offended Californians. They were called "dumb Okies" by the Californians.

Some of the Okies lived in a farm-labor camp located near the town of Arvin in the San Joaquin Valley in central California. When John Steinbeck visited the Okies in this camp, he saw starving children and sickness everywhere. Some of the Okie children were dying of starvation while farmers refused to give them surplus crops to eat. Steinbeck called this "a crime that goes beyond denunciation."

In 1939 Steinbeck published a novel called *The Grapes of Wrath*, which focused attention on the poverty of the Okies. It tells the fictional story of the Joad family, who are evicted from their farm in Sallisaw, Oklahoma. The Joads pile into an old jalopy and head west on Route 66 for California. On arriving in California, they suffer hunger, poverty, and misery. Unable to find work or a place to live, the Joads move into the farm-labor camp near Arvin and there they remain with little hope for the future.

Within three weeks of publication *The Grapes of Wrath* hit the best-seller lists, and by the end of the year 500,000 copies had been sold, an astonishing number. Since then, fourteen million copies have been sold. Today many teachers at universities call *The Grapes of Wrath* the greatest American novel ever written. However, back in 1939 there were many who disagreed with this conclusion.

The publication of *The Grapes of Wrath* caused a bitter controversy. Farmers in California denounced it, saying it was one-sided in favor of the Okies. Others said it was obscene. After he read the book, Oklahoma Congressman Lyle Boren called it "the black, infernal creation of a twisted, distorted mind." Soon there was a movement to ban *The Grapes of Wrath*. Libraries and school boards across the country refused to buy the book because it contained profanity. In August 1939, in Kern County, where the Arvin camp was located, the board of supervisors removed the book from all county libraries, saying it was "untrue." One hundred twelve people were waiting to read it at the time.

The story you are about to read occurred when *The Grapes of Wrath* was being banned, and it occurred in the camp near Arvin where Steinbeck visited the Okies. It is a true story, and it starts on the plains of Oklahoma when the sky was red and the land was being carried away by the winds of despair.

John Steinbeck.

ONE

Mean Clouds

*L*ife had always been hard on the farmers who lived in Oklahoma, and in the 1930s it was especially hard on those who lived in the Panhandle, a barren stretch of rock and red soil sandwiched between Texas, Kansas, and New Mexico. These people owned small family farms of forty to eighty acres and were "dry farmers." They had no irrigation system, no reservoirs to store water, no canals to bring water to their farms. When there was enough rain, the Okies in the Panhandle grew wheat and corn and raised cattle. When there wasn't enough rain, they were forced to sell their livestock and farm machinery and borrow money from the bank. Every year they gambled with their lives, hoping for enough rain to get by.

In 1931 it stopped raining in the Panhandle. The sky became bright and hot, and it stayed that way every day. Cornstalks in the fields shriveled from the sizzling heat. Shoots of wheat dried up and fell to the ground. The farmers were caught in an impossible situation. They were already suffering from the effects of the Great Depression, which had started in 1929 when the stock market collapsed. The Depression caused the price of wheat and corn to fall so low that it made growing these crops unprofitable. Most farmers had borrowed money to buy their land and had borrowed again against their land in lean years. When the prices for their crops fell, many couldn't make payments to the banks that held title to their land. By 1932 one thousand families a week in Texas, Oklahoma, and Arkansas were losing their farms to the banks. And now it had stopped raining in the Panhandle, and the crops themselves were failing.

*The tractor and house of a dry
farmer in Oklahoma.*

*Farming in Oklahoma. Drought
and wind have ruined the field
behind the farmer.*

Then when it seemed that things couldn't get any worse, they
did. The year was 1936. It hadn't rained more than a few drops in
the Panhandle for five straight years. One day the wind started to
blow, and every day it blew harder and harder, as if nature were
playing a cruel joke on the Okies. The wind blew the dry soil into
the air, and every morning the sun rose only to disappear behind a
sky of red dirt and dust. The wind knocked open doors, shattered
windows, and leveled barns.

It became known as the great Dust Bowl, and it was centered in
the Panhandle near Goodwell, Oklahoma. From there it stretched

to the western half of Kansas, the eastern half of Colorado, the northeastern portion of New Mexico, and northern Texas. In these areas, and especially in the Panhandle, the dry winds howled for four long years, from 1936 to 1940. Frequently the wind blew more than fifty miles an hour, carrying away the topsoil and leaving only hard red clay, which made farming impossible.

The
Dust Bowl,
1936–1940

NEBRASKA

COLORADO

KANSAS

• Kansas City

MISSOURI

• Wichita

Goodwell

NEW

MEXICO

Oklahoma
Panhandle

• Oklahoma City

OKLAHOMA

ARKANSAS

• Dallas

LOUISIANA

TEXAS

• Austin

Houston •

DUST BOWL

AREA OF DETAIL

March 1936: A dust storm rises over the Texas Panhandle. Horace Ray Conley of Foss, Oklahoma, said storms like these made the sky "boil red, blood red."

In the flatlands of the Panhandle people could see the dust storms coming from twenty to thirty miles away. The winds made the sky "boil red, blood red," said Horace Ray Conley of Foss, Oklahoma. "You could see the northers coming," he recalled. "It carried that old red dirt, and the whole sky would be red. They were mean clouds, ugly clouds." As a child, Horace walked to school backward to keep the dirt from scraping him in the face. He remembered he was often let out of school to go to the family storm cellar where he would be safe.

As the clouds rose and roiled each day, thousands of birds and rabbits raced in front of the approaching storms. That was the signal to the Okies to hurry before it was too late. They had to herd their cows into the barn quickly, tie down farm equipment and whatever supplies they had outside, then run for cover. Cracks around windows and doors were taped or stuffed with wet towels, but it was impossible to escape the dust. At night families slept with wet washcloths or sponges over their faces to filter out the dust, but in the morning they would find their pillows and blankets caked with dirt, their tongues and teeth coated with grit.

Every morning the house had to be cleaned. Everett Buckland of Waynocka said, "If you didn't sweep the dust out right quick between the storms, you'd end up scooping it out with a shovel." And every morning someone had to go check the animals. The fierce gales buried chickens, pigs, dogs, and occasionally cattle. Children were assigned the task of cleaning the nostrils of cows two or three times a day.

An Oklahoma farmer and his son raising the height of a fence to keep it from being buried by drifts of blowing soil.

Sometimes drifting soil buried highways. A laborer clears a road near Guymon, in the Oklahoma Panhandle.

The storms also created a charge of free-flowing static electricity in the air. If you touched anything metal—a frying pan, a pump handle, a doorknob—you could get a jolting shock. Some old-timers even say the static power electrocuted dozens of jackrabbits.

The Dust Bowl killed people who stayed out too long without shelter. Roland Hoeme of Hooker almost lost his grandmother to one storm. "I remember my grandmother hanging on to a fence post," he said. "The wind was blowin' so hard she looked like a pennant in a breeze." However, more people died from "dust pneumonia"—when the dust caused severe damage to the lungs. Bessie Zentz of Goodwell summed up the nightmare experienced by the "Dust Bowlers," as they came to be called: "The dust storms scared us to pieces," Bessie said. "It was dark as the middle of the night, and it stayed that way all day."

*The children of an Oklahoma
farmer, 1939.*

The storms ended any hope of farming in the Panhandle. The Okies planted mulberry trees for windbreaks and plowed furrows deep in the ground to help keep the soil in place. But the wind blasted the seeds from the furrows and whipped the crops from the earth. To survive, farmers took to hunting jackrabbits, and the Panhandle diet became biscuits, beans, and "fried jack." Others took to hunting coyote, not to eat but to collect the bounty offered by the state for each one killed.

It was a time of desperation. From 1930 to 1940 the number of farmers and agricultural workers in the Dust Bowl states declined by approximately 400,000; by 1937 the unemployment rate in Oklahoma, Arkansas, and Texas had soared to 30 percent. Most of the Okies had lost their farms or were about to; nearly 50 percent of Oklahoma's farms changed hands in bankruptcy court sales in the 1930s. When a farmer couldn't pay the bank, a tractor was sent to knock down his farmhouse as a way of forcing him to leave the land—"tractored out," they called it. The Okies were broke, they were without land, and they were hungry. And still the wind blew day and night, scraping all life from the earth. It's little wonder that Okies named this period in their lives the Dirty Thirties.

TWO

Mother Road

The Okies drew strength from the winds that blew them out of the Panhandle. Penniless, broken by hardship and poverty, they were determined to conquer adversity. Crowding around campfires on the open prairie amid the ruins of their farmhouses and fields, they started to talk about a distant place where, it was reported, there was food, work, sunshine—and clear skies.

California! California! California! To the Okies the word "California" was magical, describing a place where they could go to better their lives. It was said that thousands of workers were needed to harvest a hundred different crops—peaches, pears, tomatoes, potatoes, beans, apples, oranges—the list seemed endless. It was said that no one ever went hungry in California because lush orchards were everywhere and people just helped themselves to whatever fruits or vegetables they wanted. It was said that no one ever got sick out there, ever, and it was big news if anyone died in California before their 200th birthday!

Above all, the Dust Bowlers believed they would find work in California—if they could get there. They believed this because growers in California sent thousands of handbills to Oklahoma and the other Dust Bowl states, handbills that said things like 300 WORKERS NEEDED FOR PEACHES—PLENTY OF WORK—HIGH WAGES and 500 MEN FOR COTTON—NEEDED NOW!—START WORK RIGHT AWAY! When the Okies read these advertisements nailed on trees and old telephone poles, there was but one thing to do. As one man in Porum, Oklahoma, put it, "All you could hear was 'Goin' to Californ-I-A! Goin' to Californ-I-A!' Nobody talked about nothin' else 'cept goin' to Californ-I-A!"

The advertisements for workers led to what is called the Dust Bowl migration. It was the largest migration of people in U.S. history. Between 1935 and 1940 over one million people left their homes in Oklahoma, Texas, Arkansas, and Missouri and moved to California. Most of the migrants were white, but the exodus from the southwestern states also included some black families. Among the migrants, 375,000 Okies cursed the wind, the dirt, and the drought one last time, then set out for "Californ-I-A."

And what a sight it was! The Okies sold what few valuable possessions they still had: an old tractor, a plow, perhaps a cow that had survived. Then aunts and uncles, brothers and sisters, parents and grandparents, pooled their money to buy an old jalopy, or a beat-up flatbed truck. Soon the vehicle would be loaded down with

The Elmer Thomas family of Muskogee, Oklahoma, before leaving their home for the last time.

tools, pots, pans, bulging suitcases, guitars, washtubs, and mattresses. And always, straddling the ten-foot-high mountain of family possessions, there were children, often six or more, whose job it was to make sure the ropes stayed tight and nothing was lost.

For others there was nothing to sell, nothing to pack. Many of these Okies "rode the rail" to California, sneaking aboard empty railroad boxcars heading west. Some, such as Roy Abbot of Coalgate, hitchhiked to California. "Moving day," Roy said, "consisted of callin' the dog and spittin' on the fire." For those with their own vehicles, an old car with three mattresses lashed to its roof was called "rich." A car with two mattresses was said to be "mediocre." And if someone saw a car with just one mattress, they'd say, "There goes a *poor Okie*."

Migrant families sold many of their possessions and packed the rest into old cars and trucks for the journey west. This family from Kansas took their goat with them.

While preparing for the trip of nearly two thousand miles, which might take them from three weeks to six months, many Okie families sang the popular Jack Bryant song "Sunny Cal":

You've all heard the story
Of old Sunny Cal
The place where it never rains
They say it don't know how.
They say, "Come on, you Okies,"
Work is easy found
Bring along your cotton sack
You can pick the whole year round.

Route 66,
"Mother Road"

Then one by one the overloaded trucks sputtered onto Route 66, which Okies called Mother Road. Today, most of old Route 66 is closed or in a state of disrepair. But the Okies who rode Mother Road to California will never forget the blast-furnace heat, the winding mountain roads, the bridgeless rocky paths, the washed-out mud banks, the hunger, and the uncertainty that threatened them every mile of the way. When Okies recall the Dust Bowl migration, they remember every town: first Shamrock and Amarillo in northern Texas, then Tucumcari and Albuquerque in New Mexico; on to Holbrook, Flagstaff, and Kingman in Arizona, and then Needles and Barstow as they entered California. They remember every hardship and every happy moment.

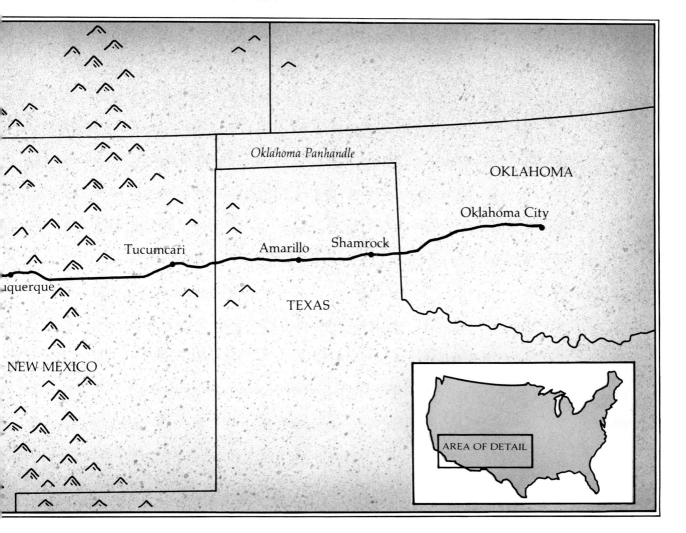

◆ MOTHER
ROAD

*A migrant family's truck, loaded
down with pots, furniture, and other
possessions.*

Edgar and Myrtle Masters packed their children in an old
Studebaker in Hollis, Oklahoma, and headed down Mother Road in
1938; they had four flat tires in the first fifty miles. Rosalene Long
was nine years old when her family of five and "a cranky young
couple with a loud toddler" left Stuart, Oklahoma. Rosalene
remembered that the family got caught in a flood in Gallup, New
Mexico, and was forced to hide out for a week in a large tin building
with twelve other families until the floodwaters subsided.

The Okies worked along the way. They might pick cotton in
Twitty, Texas, to earn enough money to get to Wikieup, Arizona,
in time for the lettuce and carrot harvest. If their truck broke down

or they ran out of money for gas, which happened often, some of the men would hitchhike to the nearest town, get an odd job and maybe earn fifty cents, enough money for repairs or gas for the next day.

At the end of the day the families would camp by the side of the road and wash clothes, if there was a stream or ditch nearby. They ate sugar-cured bacon brought from Oklahoma stuffed in lard cans, and if they were lucky, they had a meal of boiled potatoes and carrots. They cooked outside, slept outside, went to the bathroom in the woods, bathed when they could, and did whatever it took to get to the next day. Lloyd Searcy's family—eight boys and four

Three families from Oklahoma pulled up along the highway in New Mexico because of a broken-down car. They are looking for work picking cotton. "Would go back to Oklahoma," one of the migrants told the photographer, "but can't get along there."

*A migrant family washes up at a
hot spring in the California desert.*

girls—slept outside next to Mother Road. "With all of our blankets
and sleeping bags," Lloyd said, "we looked like a checkerboard all
laid out." Comparing the trip to life in Prague, Oklahoma, Lloyd
said, "We didn't have no running water or electricity, but we didn't
have that in Oklahoma either." Loye Stoops of Chicota
remembered when his family ran out of food and all that was left
was coffee. The coffee was shared by the adults, then the children
took spoons and ate the coffee grounds.

Once the Okie families reached Kingman in western Arizona,
they faced a new challenge. From Kingman, Route 66 wound
upward into the cactus and shattered rock of the Black Mountains.
As this stretch of Mother Road climbed higher and higher, the
steep grade, the hairpin turns, and the absence of guardrails tested
every vehicle and the determination of each family. Women and

*A family pulled over to the side of
the road in California, seven months
after leaving their home in
Missouri.*

children often walked to the summit rather than face the perilous climb in an unreliable car. They carried washtubs and bundles of clothing to ease the strain on the family's jalopy. Horace Ray Conley, who had described the sky above the Panhandle as "blood red," was fifteen when his father's 1930 ton and a half truck approached the foothills of the Black Mountains. It was loaded with two beds, a stove, a dining table, and a couch. When his father refused to take the wheel, Horace shifted the old truck into low gear and started up the grade alone. He climbed about a mile before the truck's clutch failed. Two truckers from Maine fed cantaloupes to the Conley family and gave them a ride back to one of the many gas stations in Kingman.

Once through the Black Mountains, the Okies had to prepare for their most severe test, crossing 143 miles of the Mojave Desert

*Opposite: A migrant boy plays his guitar
and sings while camped by the roadside.*

between Needles and Barstow, California. Here there were no towns and few gas stations. Here fan belts snapped, radiators cracked, and floorboards turned frying-pan hot in daytime temperatures that frequently exceeded 120 degrees. The families prepared for this part of the trip as if they were going into battle, checking tires and brakes, securing extra food, gas, and water. Most made the journey at night and always at a slow speed, keeping a steady eye on the temperature gauge. "I use to tell them," a local businessman said of the Okies, "it isn't surprising that you people die along Route 66. The miracle is that any of you make it through at all."

To help survive the hardest times, the Okies wrote songs. As they joined the caravan of rundown jalopies on Mother Road, they would sing,

> *If the day looks kinder gloomy*
> *An' the chances kinder slim;*
> *If the situation's puzzlin',*
> *An' the prospect awful grim,*
> *An' perplexities keep pressin'*
> *Till all hope is nearly gone*
> *Just bristle up and grit your teeth,*
> *An' keep on going on.*

Another song, "Goin' Down the Road Feelin' Bad," went like this:

> *I'm goin' down the road feelin' bad,*
> *I'm goin' down the road feelin' bad,*
> *I'm goin' down the road feelin' bad,*
> *Lawd, Lawd,*
> *And I ain't gonna be treated this-a-way.*

Always they kept up hope: hope that the truck wouldn't overheat again, hope that the tires would last one more day, hope that there would be enough food and water for tomorrow, hope that they would eventually "'light" in California, and above all, hope that they could find a job when they got there.

◆

THREE
Dead Time

The winding stream of Dust Bowl jalopies eventually reached Tehachapi Grade. It is a beautiful road that snakes gently through the Tehachapi Mountains of California, then shoots straight down to the San Joaquin Valley like a dangerous ski slope. For the Okie families who descended the grade, it was a time of rejoicing and laughter. All of their troubles suddenly seemed to disappear, for now they could see with their own eyes what they had only dreamed about for months, sometimes years. From two thousand feet above sea level they saw a vast stretch of orchards, endless fields of grapes, cotton, and tomatoes, and as far as the eye could see in any direction, green—so much green it was hard to believe after life in the Panhandle.

"It was paradise," Trice Masters recalled. "When we saw the valley we started hollerin' and yellin' 'cause we knew it was Californ'. We started singin' and we didn't care. If we ran out of gas we'd make it 'cause we could coast down." When Patsy Lamb's family saw the valley for the first time through the windshield of their old Model A Ford, her father pulled the car off to the side of the road on a high bluff. Patsy and her four brothers and sisters got out of the car and stood in a line on the edge of the bluff, where they stared at the sea of green below them as if in a trance. Patsy was ten years old at the time. When she turned away from the bluff, she saw her mother standing behind her crying. Then Patsy started to cry, and soon everyone was crying.

From 1935 to 1940 an endless stream of ramshackle cars and trucks rolled down Tehachapi Grade. Patsy Lamb's family and the other migrants from the Dust Bowl states poured into the

The Tehachapi Mountains, California, 1939.

agricultural towns in the southern end of the San Joaquin Valley—Delano and Bakersfield, where the advertisements said grape pickers were needed; Wasco and Shafter, where it was said field hands were needed for potatoes; Arvin and Lamont, where rumor had it that work could be found harvesting cotton, carrots, and beans. But the Okies soon discovered they had been misled about California. They started seeing signs at the edge of every town they approached: NO JOBS HERE! IF YOU ARE LOOKING FOR WORK—KEEP OUT! 10 MEN FOR EVERY JOB!

Everywhere they went it was the same—too many workers and not enough jobs. The growers in California had advertised for more workers than they actually needed, so there was a surplus of farm labor. This suited the growers, because the excess of workers drove wages down. A grower would offer to hire someone for

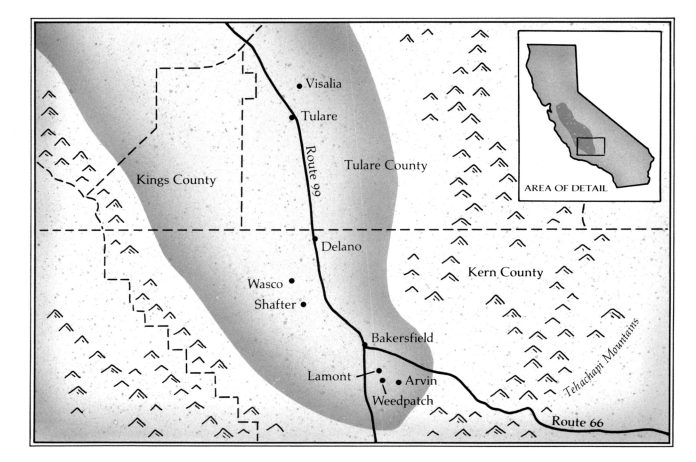

The southern San Joaquin Valley, 1936

twenty-five cents an hour to pick cotton, a poverty wage. If the migrant didn't take the job because his family couldn't live on twenty-five cents an hour, there were a thousand other workers who *would* pick cotton for twenty-five cents an hour to keep *their* families from starving. The growers offered thirty-five cents an hour for plums and nectarines, twenty cents for potatoes and lettuce, and a starvation wage of two and a half cents for a box of peaches—*one dollar* for a *ton* of peaches. The average field hand worked sixteen hours a day, seven days a week, and earned four dollars a week. But most Okie laborers couldn't find work for even a nickel a day.

What California had to offer the Okies was more hunger and misery. In a pamphlet John Steinbeck wrote before publishing *The Grapes of Wrath*, he described the hardships the Okies faced during their first few months in California. He called it dead time.

Agricultural workers in the San Joaquin Valley.

There is no work. First the gasoline gives out. And without gasoline a man cannot go to a job if he could get one. Then the food goes. And then it rains, with insufficient food, the children develop colds because the ground in the tents is wet. I talked to a man last week who lost two children in ten days with pneumonia. His face was hard and fierce and he didn't talk much.

During dead time, the Okies lived in the bottoms of dry lakes such as Kern Lake and Buena Park Lake in tents and shacks made out of cardboard and tin. Others lived on ditch banks, under bridges, and in fields of weed and rock. These squatter communities became known as Little Oklahomas or Okievilles, and the people who lived in them had no work and nothing to eat except boiled cabbage and corn bread. California was one of the richest agricultural states in the nation, yet Okie children were starving.

LUTHER LIBRARY
MIDLAND COLLEGE
FREMONT, NE 68025

An Okie mother and her two children in a squatter camp, or "Little Oklahoma," in 1936. Their broken-down car still has its Oklahoma license plate.

Opposite: A migrant woman, recently widowed and the mother of six children, in an "Okieville" in 1936. This photograph, taken by Dorothea Lange, was widely published and, like John Steinbeck's novel The Grapes of Wrath, *drew the attention of the American public to the plight of the Okies in California.*

The farms often produced more than could be picked or sold, but if the Okies tried to help themselves to the surplus crop left on the ground, the growers might pour oil on the food, strike a match, and set the crop on fire, hoping the Okies would move on to another town. John Steinbeck saw this happen several times and called it the "saddest, bitterest thing of all."

Inevitably, disease broke out in the Okievilles scattered throughout the San Joaquin Valley. The bad sanitary conditions and inadequate diet led to epidemics of dysentery, tuberculosis, and pneumonia. "Even if we found work," one squatter said, "the people starved. We lived like animals."

The stories Okies tell about living in the squalor and filth of these camps are shocking and tragic. For example, when Nelda Oldham and her seven-month-old brother arrived in California

from Ringling, Oklahoma, both fell ill with dysentery. Nelda recovered in five days, just in time to attend her brother's funeral. Six months after arriving in California, Lillian Dunn's seventeen-month-old son, Donald Ray, ate a frostbitten orange that was part of the family's wages for working in an orange grove. Donald got sick, and Lillian took him to Tulare County Hospital for treatment. But the hospital said it didn't take "Okies," and it refused to admit him. Donald died.

Two toddlers bathe in a rusty tin tub at a roadside camp. Poor sanitary conditions in the squatter camps led to outbreaks of disease.

Eventually a rumor spread throughout the squatter camps, a rumor that, if true, might lead to a better life for the Okies. It was said that the federal government was building several farm-labor camps where Okies could live until they found work. It was one of the few rumors Okies heard in California that turned out to be true. In 1936 the Farm Security Administration, an agency of the Department of Agriculture, started to build twelve camps in the San Joaquin Valley. By 1937 ten of these camps had been completed. They were built to provide the Okies with emergency shelter and better living conditions. One of these compounds was named Arvin Federal Camp, located at the base of Tehachapi Grade about fifteen miles south of Bakersfield near the towns of Arvin and Weedpatch. Because it was situated on Weedpatch Highway, the Okies called this place Weedpatch Camp; so did John Steinbeck in *The Grapes of Wrath*. When the Okies heard the rumor about the camp, they knocked down their cardboard shacks, packed their pots, pans, washtubs, and mattresses once again and headed back to the foothills of the Tehachapi Mountains, where they had first seen California through tears of joy.

Penniless migrants from Oklahoma on a highway in California. "Can't make it," this man told the photographer. "Want to go back. Ate up our car. Ate up our tent. Living like hogs."

Two views of Arvin Federal Camp, or "Weedpatch Camp," as it came to be known. The tall buildings in the background of each photograph are the camp's sanitation units.

Weedpatch Camp was no paradise, but for the families who settled there it was a vast improvement over life in an Okieville. The camp housed about three hundred people in one-room tin cabins and tents on wooden platforms. It cost one dollar a week to live there, but if a family didn't have a dollar—and many didn't—they could work off the cost of the rent by doing maintenance work around the camp. Jason Johnson traded his car jack for a tank of gas, which he used to find two days' work unloading lumber from a railroad car. He made a dollar and a half—enough to move his family into the camp. Patsy Lamb's family got in by selling ten sacks of potatoes her family had somehow "acquired."

The camp had hot showers, flush toilets, and breakfast for the children for one penny a day. Their parents could earn this much by finding occasional work in the fields or by doing odd jobs in Arvin and Lamont. On those occasions when the Okies weren't paid in money, they worked for a cup of flour and a spoonful of lard, which

would make biscuits for the family meal. When it rained, the tents and tin cabins leaked and Weedpatch Camp turned into a swamp of mud. Weeks might go by without finding even the poorest-paying job. But friendships were strong in the camp, and someone would always share a standard meal of "bean an' biscuit." Life seemed a bit better too because right in the middle of Weedpatch Camp there was a makeshift auditorium constructed of scrap lumber that was used as a dance hall on Saturday nights.

Here families would gather to sing and "pick," playing an odd assortment of instruments that clattered and twanged—spoon, washboard, saw, and of course banjo, harmonica, fiddle, and guitar. They sang the Okie tunes that gave them identity and strength, for the people in Weedpatch Camp had learned to accept hardship without showing weakness. "Now, come on, everybody, quit that complaining," one woman said. "Every cloud has a silver lining. If you don't like things here in camp, be nice enough to keep it to yourself." " 'Tain't no use to sit an' whine," one song advised, while another, "Tow-Sack Tattler," went like this:

It takes a little courage;
And a little self-control;
And a grim determination;
If you want to reach the goal;

It takes a deal of striving;
And a firm and stern-set chin;
No matter what the battle,
If you really want to win.

You must take a blow and give one.
You must risk and you must lose
And expect with the battle
You must suffer from a bruise.

But you mustn't wince or falter
Lest a fight you might begin.
Be a man and face the battle.
That's the only way to win.

A Saturday night dance in March 1940 at the Tulare Camp for migrant workers. The Tulare Camp, about eighty miles north of Arvin, was one of several built by the federal government. Like Weedpatch Camp, it had a makeshift auditorium and dance hall, where families gathered to entertain themselves.

The Okies would need all the courage and toughness they could find. Weedpatch Camp provided shelter and better sanitation for the Okies who lived there. But outside the camp they still faced an uncertain future.

As well as shelter, Weedpatch Camp provided the Okies who lived there with basic health care. This woman, who had tuberculosis, received daily visits from a Kern County nurse.

✦

Opposite:
In February 1936, the Los Angeles Police Department sent over 130 officers to points along the California state line to turn back hitchhikers, riders on freight trains, and travelers without jobs or means of support. These patrols, intended to stop the flood of migrants into California, became known as the "Bum Blockade." Here police turn back a group of men on a bridge at the California-Arizona border.

FOUR

"Okie, Go Home!"

When they left Weedpatch Camp to find work, the Okies faced ridicule, rejection, and shame. "Okie use' ta mean you was from Oklahoma," an Okie says in *The Grapes of Wrath*. "Now it means you're a dirty son-of-a-bitch. Okie means you're scum." A store owner in nearby Arvin called Okies "ignorant, filthy people." A local doctor said they were "shiftless trash who lived like dogs." One woman screamed, "There's more darn 'Okies' in California than white people," while a local newspaper, the *Kern Herald*, alarmed readers with the headline MIGRANT HORDE INVADES KERN.

Californians were hostile to Okies because they competed with residents for jobs and because taxpayers were forced to pay for problems that arose as a result of the Okie migration to California. For example, epidemics of disease in the Okievilles caused the health and sanitation budget for Kern County to double between 1935 and 1940. During the same period, overcrowding in the schools caused Kern County's education bill to increase by 214 percent, while property taxes rose 50 percent.

When an Okie family went to downtown Bakersfield, they saw signs on store windows reading OKIES—GO SHOPPING SOMEWHERE ELSE and NO OKIES ALLOWED! If an Okie family could save enough money to go to the Fox movie theater in Bakersfield—which few could—they would see a sign outside reading OKIES—SIT IN THE BALCONY! Elyse Phillips of Broken Bow, Oklahoma, who was nine at the time, said that everywhere her family went they would hear shouts of "Okie, go home!" "They never said it right to your face. They would stand behind you on a street or yell it at you from a car." But what hurt her the most were the "Okie jokes" that made

Despite hardship and the hostility of Californians, Okies remained proud and determined to conquer adversity. "Yes'm, we're getting along just fine," this Okieville resident told the photographer.

fun of the way her family looked and talked, as if they weren't even human beings. Elyse especially hated the joke about an Okie cotton picker: When a father identified a man in a field as an Okie cotton picker, his son said, "Daddy, them things look almost like people when they stand on their legs, don't they?"

Okies stood out because of their visible poverty and because they talked in the twang and drawl of the people from the Dust Bowl states. They used "ain't" and "might could" and dropped the letter *g* from the end of most words, saying "playin'," "singin'," and "pickin'." They said "saaat" instead of "sat" and "doawg" instead of "dog." Because they spoke differently and wore shabby clothes, the Okies couldn't hide who they were, even if they wanted to, and surely there were times when some Okies wished they weren't Okies. Perhaps Jack Atkison was one: "They classified you as an

'Okie.' They didn't want you. You were an outcast. You was no good." Perhaps Mae McMasters wished she had been born somewhere else: "People acted like we was dirt under their feet." Perhaps Shirley Cox wanted to be anyone other than an Okie newly arrived from the Panhandle. Shirley was sitting with her mother and brother in front of a store in Porterville. Suddenly, "This man came out of the store and yelled at us, 'You Okies get out of here! I don't know what you Okies are doing here. Get out!' My mom just sat there and cried."

To some of the people who lived in Weedpatch Camp, "Okie" was a "fightin' word." They were proud of who they were, proud to have endured such hardships, proud enough to fight back. LeRoy Collins went to jail for getting into a fistfight with a man in a

Many of the residents of Weedpatch Camp were children. This woman had twenty-two grandchildren, three of whom appear in this photograph.

hardware store who called LeRoy's family "a bunch of dumb Okies." Beth Stewart remembered that her husband, Cory, got into a fight when he went to find a job at a cannery. Hundreds of men were lined up for work, and when Cory saw a sign at the cannery's office reading NO JOBS FOR OKIES, he got angry, ripped the sign off the wall, and got into a brawl with three security guards. A popular poem at the time sums up what Okies thought about the people who shouted "Okie, go home!"

> Some of the Californians go around
> with their nose stuck up;
> Like when it would rain,
> They'd use it for a cup.

But the feeling of rejection was greatest among Okie children. Because they had been poor for so long and had been traveling for months to get to California, the Okie children had not been able to attend school, and many couldn't read or write. When they went to school each day, most of the teachers ignored the migrants,

An Okie child with a cotton sack at Weedpatch Camp, 1936.

believing that Okie kids were too stupid to learn the alphabet, too dumb to master math, and too "retarded" to learn much of anything. Other teachers forced the newcomers to sit on the floor in the back of the classroom, while the non-Okie kids, well dressed with clean faces and the best school supplies, sat at desks and poked fun at their classmates who wore dresses made out of chicken-feed sacks, baggy overalls held up by rope, and frequently no shoes at all.

"Okie kids," said Eddie Davis, who was twelve at the time, "were the scum of the earth." The girls were called "maggie" and "maggot," a play on the word "migrant." The boys were humiliated when the school nurse checked them for lice. Wayne Rogers remembered, "As she looked through our hair and our ears she would tell us, 'Okies have lice. Okies have lice.' That made me feel terrible." Ruth Criswell recalled, "Every day, my daughters were jeered in school as Okies. My oldest girl would come home so mad every day she could hardly stand it." Myrle Dansby, a twelve-year-old, wrote a poem to express her sense of humiliation:

> The teachers nag
> And look at you
> Like a dirty dish rag.

One Okie father described what it was like for the Okie children in these words:

> Picture how you would feel with two or three children headed for school, almost barefoot, with ragged or ill-fitting clothing. You see them going down the road with a paper bag in their hands, with two baking-powder biscuits, maybe, and some beans in between. And if you were a little child, how would you feel going to school that way—and when it comes noon you sit down in your little bunch and drag out those two sandwiches full of beans, when the rest of the little ones are sitting around you there, children of more fortunate people? How do the children feel? How would you feel?

But like their parents, the Okie children drew strength from one another. They were tough and they believed they could be as good as anyone else if they were just given a chance. That chance came along in the form of a kind man who was standing in a field of dirt just next to Weedpatch Camp.

FIVE

Mr. Hart

*L*eo Hart liked to visit the Okie children when they played in the field next to Weedpatch Camp. He was forty years old at the time, but it did not seem unusual to the children that this tall, slender man came to their makeshift playground at least once a week. When he played tag or baseball with the Okie kids or sat in a circle with them in the field and talked, the children called him Mr. Hart. He was a caring man who always had a smile on his face, as if he knew some great secret no one else knew.

Leo took off his suit coat and tie and went barefoot with the Okie kids. He listened to them talk about the "terror wind" in the Panhandle, about eating carrot stems and apple pits along Mother Road, and about the ridicule they faced in town and in school. "He knew what we were goin' through," Joyce Foster recalled. "He knew they called us maggots and scum. He understood and he cared." Like Joyce, who was ten at the time, all the children looked forward to seeing "Mr. Hart"—but none of them could have guessed what the man in the dirt field had in store for them.

Leo had been born and raised in Vinton, Iowa, where his mother was a teacher in a rural school and his father operated a plumbing business from a horse-drawn wagon. As a young man, Leo joined the United States Army and fought in France during World War I. Before the end of the war, he contracted tuberculosis and almost died. Doctors sent him to a sanitarium in the hot, dry climate of Tucson, Arizona, hoping he would recover. He did, barely—after surgeons removed a lung and a kidney.

Leo checked out of the hospital and enrolled as a student at the University of Arizona, where he earned a master's degree in education and met his lifelong companion and future wife, Edna. In 1927, Leo took his first teaching position, in Bakersfield, California. By 1938, when Okie children were crowding into the schools of Kern County, Leo was head counselor in the Kern County High School District. "Every day," he recalled, "I talked to a dozen children who were crying because someone had called them a dumb Okie." It was as head counselor—and as playmate in the field next to Weedpatch Camp—that Leo came to know the problems facing the Okie children and decided to take action.

In 1939 Leo decided to run for the office of Kern County superintendent of education. He was well known and had advised most of the students and made friends with their parents at PTA meetings, so it was no surprise that he was elected. But Leo knew that most people in Kern County would fight any attempt to help the Okies, so it was no surprise either that during his campaign he avoided saying anything about helping Okie kids in the public schools.

"The big problem for me," the superintendent said, "was to find out what to do for these children to get them adjusted into society and to take their *rightful place*." Leo knew that many of the Okie kids were illiterate. He knew that they ate with their fingers and went to the bathroom outdoors and needed, as Leo put it, training in "manners, morals, and etiquette." He knew that most were undernourished and needed medical attention, not to mention shirts, dresses, and shoes. And he knew that the Okie children knew all of this too and cried—or fought back with their fists—when they were called dumb Okies. But because he played and talked with the Okie children he also knew that they were "ordinary kids," Leo said, "with the same hopes and dreams the rest of us have." Leo believed that with hard work, with determination, and with a belief in themselves, the children of Weedpatch Camp could take their "rightful place."

It would not be an easy task. When Leo was elected superintendent, hostility in Kern County toward Okies was at a fever pitch. Policemen and civilians formed armed patrols called Bum Brigades and guarded the county's borders to keep Okies out. In 1938 a mob headed by the sheriff burned down an Okie migrant camp under the Kern River Bridge. Then irate farmers armed with pitchforks,

Leo Hart.

Okie children, Weedpatch Camp, 1936—"ordinary kids," Leo Hart said, "with the same hopes and dreams the rest of us have."

guns, bricks, and clubs attacked Weedpatch Camp at night and tried to drive the Okies out. (Hundreds of Okies went to jail for defending themselves and their families, but not one local was arrested.) In 1939 Kern County banned *The Grapes of Wrath*.

All the while, Leo continued to visit the Okie kids in the field next to Weedpatch. During this period of violence against Okies, Patsy Lamb later recalled, "Mr. Hart was our only friend."

First Leo tried to place the Okie children in the outlying rural schools of Kern County, hoping they might blend in with the

A copy of The Grapes of Wrath *is burned by farmers in Bakersfield in 1939. The president of the Kern County farmers' association called the book "obscene" and "vile propaganda."*

sons and daughters of farmers and ranchers. But he met stiff opposition. One high-ranking school official in the Vineland School District called the superintendent's office and scolded Leo: "You're not going to spend our money for these sons-a-bitches! You can't educate these sons-a-bitches! They're going to grow up just like their fathers and mothers. They're a shiftless lot. They've got no brains!" Soon Leo's office was flooded with letters from angry parents protesting his plan. The parents demanded that Leo remove *all* Okie children from *all* the public schools. At least two educators called Leo a communist and warned that his job might be in jeopardy, even though he had held it only a few months.

The opposition to the Okie children angered Leo. Edna Hart recalled that her husband would come home from work so upset that he couldn't eat or sleep. "I could never understand," Leo said, "why these kids should be treated differently. I could never understand why they shouldn't be given the same opportunity as others. Someone had to do something for them because no one cared about them."

In 1940 Leo decided that if no one wanted the Okie kids in the public schools, then maybe the Okie children should have their own school. It would be a different school, he thought. It would be more than bricks and buildings, more than lessons and homework in math and writing. It would teach practical skills, such as masonry, mechanics, and agriculture. It would also teach the children to be proud of who they were. It would instill self-confidence in them so they might succeed in life on their own. It would provide the Okie children, Leo said, "with educational experiences in a broader and richer curriculum than were present in most schools." Above all else, Leo insisted, it would be "their school."

SIX

Weedpatch School

In April 1940 Superintendent Hart phoned the president of the Vineland school board, who was usually hostile to Okies and to the superintendent's office. But on this day Leo was phoning to tell the school board just what it wanted to hear.

Leo told the president of the board that he wanted to remove the Okie children from the public schools. The president enthusiastically agreed. Then Leo asked him to declare that an emergency existed. "The emergency," Leo said, "was overcrowding in the public schools." Knowing that the president was willing to consider any idea that might solve what he thought of as the Okie problem, Leo asked him for permission to build an "emergency school" for Okie children "at no expense to the district." Swiftly the president granted permission—without asking where this school might be located or how it might come about.

At the same time, Leo made friends with Dewey Russell, the manager of Weedpatch Camp and a close friend of John Steinbeck. In May 1940, with Dewey's help, Leo leased a ten-acre site of land from the federal government for ten dollars. It was a special piece of land: It was the field next to the camp, where Leo played with the children. Leo then declared that a school existed in this field—Arvin Federal Emergency School, or as it came to be called, Weedpatch School. And so Weedpatch School started with no grass, no sidewalks, no playground equipment, no toilets, no water, no books, no teachers. It started, Leo remembered, with two condemned buildings that had been in the field for years and with "fifty poorly clad, undernourished, and skeptical youngsters."

In May and June, Leo visited several colleges and universities in

Leo Hart (on the left, holding his hat) with some of the staff of Weedpatch School, including principal Pete Bancroft (fourth from left, wearing a suit jacket) and Charlene McGee (second from right). Edna Hart is standing in the center, with her coat draped over her shoulders.

California and sought out, as he put it, "the best teachers . . . teachers whose attitude indicated that they were really interested in this type of student and wanted to help in the program."

Jim McPherson, who was working on his doctorate degree at the time, agreed to come, even after Leo told Jim he would have to teach history, geography, math, *and* science, and all "at a basic level." Charlene McGee agreed to come, even though she would have to teach the three R's, plus health and animal husbandry. Rose Gilger, Beverly Ahrens, Barbara Sabovitch, and Marie Marble all came knowing they would be teaching science, chemistry, typing—and also working as cooks in the cafeteria. And Lee Hanson's duties would include teaching English, plumbing, electrical wiring, sports,

and aircraft mechanics! This was what Leo meant by "a broader and richer curriculum." These people—and half a dozen more—were recruited to be teachers, carpenters, masons, field hands, common laborers, counselors—and anything else that might serve the needs of the Okie children.

Next Leo became a beggar, a borrower, a scrounger of wood and nails, books and paper, and whatever else he could lay his hands on that might be of some use. "I became a panhandler," Leo remembered, "and I was pretty good." His pitch was simple—and it was just what the residents of Kern County wanted to hear: The Dust Bowl kids would be withdrawn from the public schools and set off from the community in a separate school, which wouldn't cost the taxpayers a single cent. Weedpatch School would eliminate overcrowded classrooms and put an end to the daily brawls between Okie and non-Okie kids. The Okies would be "out of sight" at the new school next to the camp—and taxpayers wouldn't have to foot the bill for buses, lunches, playground equipment, and so on. "I had an entire speech," Leo said, "and they listened."

During the spring and summer of 1940, Leo and Edna stumped Kern County for donations of supplies and materials, hauling their cargo back to the field in a two and a half ton flatbed truck, which Leo bought with his salary as superintendent. From the National Youth Authority he secured twenty-five thousand bricks. From the Sears, Roebuck Foundation he acquired an assortment of sheep, pigs, chickens, and cows. Local nurseries donated plants and vegetables. Local ranchers gave different types of farm machinery. And the superintendent's office became crowded with a stockpile of used books and supplies that had been discarded by other schools in the district. As the summer months of 1940 passed, the ten-acre field next to Weedpatch Camp took on a strange appearance. A dozen piles of scrap lumber, pipes, and bricks grew higher toward the sky, as if they were somehow alive.

Some things will never be known about the early history of the school. One afternoon, Edna recalled, Leo came home with twenty-six new typewriters, which he stacked neatly in his den from floor to ceiling. He never told Edna where he got them, and she never asked. One morning Edna found a used hot-water heater on their front lawn. There was a crudely written note taped to it, which said simply L. HART. It was a surprise to both Edna and Leo.

Many residents of Kern County were generous in supporting "the Okie school," as they called it. But it is equally true that others opposed it and continued to shout "Okie, go home!" The Salvation Army gave Edna a mountain of clothes and shoes for the Okie children. But Leo and Edna were shunned by members of the PTA, and churchgoers refused to sit near them during Sunday services. One day there would be an unexpected gift, such as the metal lathe left in the field by someone driving a pickup truck. Then five dead cats would be discovered in the field by the Okie children. A building contractor donated fifty cans of "slightly used" paint. But as Leo was storing the paint in one of the buildings in the field, someone was slashing the tires on the flatbed truck parked in front of his house.

A piece of machinery donated by a local farmer being unloaded at the site of Weedpatch School.

It's not known who set fire to the two condemned buildings in the field, only that the Okie children extinguished the blaze before it could do much damage. And it's uncertain if some of the donations left in the field—boxes of empty cans, newspapers, assorted containers—were meant to be donations or junk dumped in a field of junk.

While Leo was making plans that summer for the start of the school, the Okie children in Weedpatch Camp picked cotton. The hot months of July and August made the cotton crop exceptionally good and meant that Okie families were needed from sunrise to sunset for three to four days a week to pluck the white bolls from their razor-sharp hulls. The long days of working in the cotton fields hardened the hands of the Okie children and gave them physical strength for the work ahead.

Adults from Weedpatch Camp contributed to the building of the school. This photograph shows men from the camp making adobe bricks, which were later used in the construction of classrooms.

◆

SEVEN
Something to Watch

On a bright September morning in 1940 the Kern County superintendent of education waved good-bye to his wife and left for work. On this day, instead of his usual coat and tie, Leo Hart was wearing old overalls and work boots. Leo told Edna he would be home late, but she already knew that. They had talked about this special day for weeks and had worked for it for months.

Leo drove the flatbed truck to the field next to Weedpatch Camp. On the odd-looking stretch of land marked by piles of bricks, boards, and boxes of whatnot, Leo met with the teachers he had hired and introduced them to the fifty children from Weedpatch Camp whose parents had agreed to let Leo have them for the day. Then he told them all to get to work. They did. Brick by brick, board by board, the children of the Dust Bowl, eight teachers, and Leo Hart built Weedpatch School.

On the first day a team of children dug a hundred-yard trench from the water tower in the camp to the condemned buildings in the field. They laid a three-quarter-inch pipe in the trench, and on the second day the school had running water. Teachers instructed the children on hygiene, while Leo and some of the boys dug two huge holes in the ground and built two outhouses. After that, Leo said, "All the children used them."

"It was something to watch," Leo remembered. "It was the first time where they were working for something of their own. It was the first time where they could be proud of who they were and what they were doing." Pete Bancroft, the newly hired principal of the school, worked side by side with the teachers and the Okie kids, building the school and instilling in the Dust Bowl children a spirit

Children laying forms for a classroom at Weedpatch School. Pete Bancroft (pointing) is giving them instructions.

of confidence and self-worth. "There was no partiality," Leo said, "no embarrassment or ridicule." Instead, "There was friendship, understanding, guidance, and love."

As the weeks stretched into months, the school rose from the field. Within two months the two condemned buildings had been renovated and made into four general-purpose classrooms. Following that, the twenty-five thousand bricks donated by the National Youth Authority were turned into three more classrooms and a cafeteria. This took an additional three months. A home economics building was needed. No problem. An old railroad car was located and moved to the school, where the boys added plumbing and wiring, and remodeled its interior. A shop building where mechanics and other trades could be learned was also needed. No problem. Leo persuaded the district to donate an

SOMETHING
TO WATCH

Students at the school learned carpentry, plumbing, and other skills.

abandoned auditorium, which was disassembled, hauled to the school, and remanufactured into a shop room. The Okie children learned a dozen useful trades—including plumbing, electrical wiring, carpentry, plastering, and masonry. Scrap lumber was sawed into bookshelves. Discarded sinks were fixed in place for a chemistry lab. Orange crates and wooden boxes were fashioned into chairs, desks, and tables.

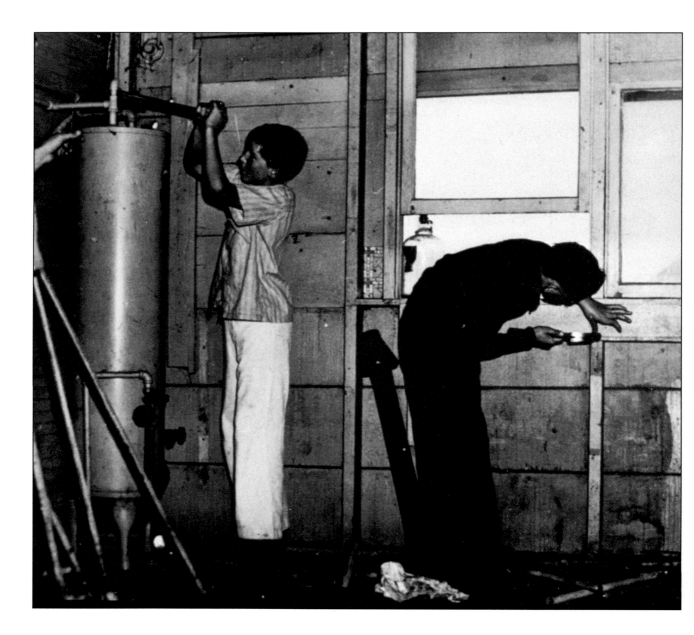

There was more. By October the field was alive with the sound of a dozen hoes and clattering farm machinery striking hard earth. The Okie children plowed part of the school field and planted vegetables and other crops. "Edna said we should start with potatoes and so we did," Leo recalled. "Potatoes and alfalfa. Tomatoes, carrots, celery, corn, and watermelon. The children especially liked the watermelon." Toiling in the sun for hours tilling, planting, weeding, and harvesting was welcome labor to children who could still remember the taste of apple seeds, carrot stems, and coffee grounds.

Scrap lumber, boxes, and orange crates were put to use and turned into shelves, desks, and chairs.

*The students at Weedpatch School
learned to operate farm machinery
and raised a variety of crops for the
school's kitchen.*

The Okie kids also raised their own livestock. They built pens for sheep, pigs, chickens, and cows and dug a basement to store slaughtered livestock. Sometime in December 1940 a local butcher heard about "the Okie school" and wandered out to the site. The man spent ten hours at the school that day slaughtering pigs and cows and instructing the children until they learned the basic skills of a butcher.

Top: Building pens for livestock.

Bottom: In late 1940, a butcher visited the school. He spent a day in the cafeteria teaching the students how to prepare livestock for the school's kitchen.

During the early months of the school, Edna Hart helped the women at Weedpatch Camp cook meals for the children. But by the time Edna went to work in the school's new cafeteria in the spring of 1941, the school had become completely self-sufficient in potatoes, vegetables, milk, eggs, and beef.

The teachers, Leo said, "went out of their way to help these children and teach them things about themselves and the world that they couldn't learn anywhere else." Jim McPherson taught the Okie children history, geography, math, science—and shoe cobbling, so they could repair their parents' shoes. Rose Gilger taught them science, typing—and sewing, so their families didn't have to wear oversize clothes or rags. Chemistry teacher Barbara Sabovitch even taught the girls how to make face cream, rouge, and lipstick—in a chemistry lab!

Principal Pete Bancroft bought a C-46 airplane from military surplus for two hundred dollars and had it carted to the school. "I taught them aircraft mechanics," Pete said, "and if they maintained a grade of 90 percent or better in arithmetic, I let them drive the plane down the makeshift runway and back." Both Pete and Leo enrolled their own children in the school and Pete brought a doctor and nurse out to care for sick children. Pete dispensed cod-liver oil

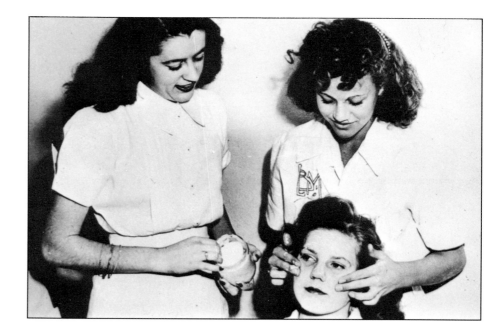

Chemistry teacher Barbara Sabovitch (left) taught the girls how to make face cream and other cosmetics in the lab. Barbara also taught typing and stenography.

Pete Bancroft leaning against the ladder of the C-46 aircraft he brought to the school. The man with a white shirt and gray hair to the left of the photograph is Dewey Russell, the manager of Weedpatch Camp.

and orange juice until the first crops came in and the school cafeteria was built. Rose Gilger and Beverly Ahrens worked in that cafeteria as well as in the classroom and, like the other teachers, took the Okie children into Bakersfield on Sundays to go to church and to accept donations of food and clothing from local merchants and the Salvation Army. Other teachers—Edith Houghan, for instance—spent weekends at the school with children who were sick, because, Edith said, "They were better off in the nurse's room than at home in their one-room huts."

Fred Smith heard about the school and applied for a job as a music teacher. Leo only had enough money to hire Fred for one day a week, but Fred usually worked on weekends for nothing. When Leo sent Fred his yearly check of six hundred dollars, Fred sent it back.

Determination and a lot of hard work combined to change the fate of the Okie children from Weedpatch Camp. As discards and donations were slowly turned into a school, the children came to believe that anything was possible—and none of them doubted this after Leo picked up a shovel one day and started to dig at the east end of the field between the school and the camp. When twelve-

The children of Weedpatch School digging what became the first public swimming pool in Kern County.

The pool in use. Weedpatch Camp is in the background.

year-old Bob Farley asked Leo what he was digging, Leo said, "Swimming pool."

If the migrant children did not "goof off," Leo said, "if they kept up on their academics," he would let them dig in their spare time. "Dig in the hole," the children called it.

"We used the twelve-by-twelve forms that were the floors of the tents over in the camp and built a wall around the inside," Leo recalled. "We poured concrete walls and a deck all the way around."

Leo made a game out of building the swimming pool during recess and after school. He helped the children set the frames and lay reinforcement rods. Then two, sometimes three wheelbarrows would be filled with cement, and Leo and the children would race the wheelbarrows to the hole in four-person teams. "The hole" became the first public swimming pool in Kern County.

When the swimming pool was finished, Elyse Phillips recalled, she pinched her nose and fell face forward into the water, "crying because I was so happy."

EIGHT

Our School

While the children of Weedpatch Camp were building a school for themselves, they were also attending classes, doing homework, and taking tests on a regular basis. Besides practical training in aircraft mechanics, sewing, cobbling, and canning fruits and vegetables, they learned the basic subjects taught in elementary school and junior high: English, arithmetic, geography, history. As many as two hundred students aged between six and sixteen attended the school during its first year of operation, from September 1940 to May 1941. Their day was divided into two three-hour periods. Half the children went to classes in the morning, normally from nine A.M. until noon, while the other half worked on building the school and tending the crops. After lunch, the groups switched places.

Sewing class.

A volleyball game during PE class.

Barbara Sabovitch's third-grade class during a lesson about transportation.

Feeding the hogs.

But it is impossible to describe a "normal" day at Weedpatch School. For example, in October 1940, twelve-year-old Doyle Powers from Ardmore, Oklahoma, was studying arithmetic with others in an unfinished classroom, which was framed with two-by-fours but had no roof. Suddenly, "The sky fell in on us. It started to rain, and classes were canceled for two days until the storm passed." In November a severe dust storm forced suspension of classes in one unfinished building when two of its walls collapsed. Della Stewart, from Duncan, Oklahoma, who was eleven, remembered missing school for nearly two weeks when her family found temporary employment in the fields of Tulare County, north of Kern. Instead of attending school every day, some children had to baby-sit siblings in the camp while adult members of the family worked.

Because attendance at the school was sometimes sporadic and because many students were learning from scratch, Leo recalled, "There were no quantum leaps in knowledge. There were only little victories, when a student understood addition or learned to write a complete sentence. But the main thing was they were learning." And they were. As weeks stretched into months and months into years, addition led to subtraction, English led to literature, and American history led to world history.

For some students at Weedpatch School, education had an immediate practical effect. For example, Joyce Foster lived with her parents and two younger brothers in two tents in Weedpatch Camp for more than three years. Joyce was ten in 1941 when she started attending the school. She was twelve when her father, thirty-six-year-old Roy Foster from Clinton, Oklahoma, contracted a lung disease while working grapes and died. Joyce cried for weeks because she missed her father. She was appointed the task of writing a letter to relatives in Clinton conveying the sad news. She was the only member of her family who could write.

Joyce also wrote an essay about her father and read it aloud to the Okie families gathered in the auditorium at Weedpatch Camp. The Okie school children sometimes read stories and poems before the dances on Saturday nights, but it was a special moment when Joyce stood on the makeshift bandstand. She remembered riding with her father on a tractor in Clinton and picking beans with him in Arizona. And as she recalled each memory she thanked her father for giving his family food, shelter, and love. Her essay was called "An Okie Man" and it was composed in an English class at Weedpatch School.

At the same time, the children who studied at Weedpatch School had life experiences they would never forget. Patsy Lamb told the story of the first Thanksgiving at the school. Leo, Edna, and the teachers prepared a turkey dinner for the children. "Mrs. Hunter

The school's cafeteria and kitchen. Students and teachers helped prepare meals, using food raised at the school.

Shop class.

told us all to go to this one big room. We were so happy," Patsy recalled. But "when we sat down and tried to eat the turkey, most of us couldn't. We never had turkey before. We didn't like the taste. We pushed the food around on our plates. Later we got some beans from the camp and we ate beans for our Thanksgiving dinner."

Other students have vivid memories of the outings at the school. On Saturdays, for students who had shown improvement and for those who scored 90 percent or better in arithmetic for the week, Leo and the teachers took the children on one-day vacations, which Leo called "outings." Nathan Reed, twelve years old out of Guymon in the Panhandle, which had few lakes or streams, caught his first fish on an outing in the Kern River Canyon. Leo's flatbed truck carried a dozen Okie children that day. The catfish were spawning in the shallows below the banks of the wild Kern River, and all of the children caught fish by hand-casting ten-foot lengths of string with hooks and worms attached. On that day, Nathan recalled, "We stayed out too long and it started to rain. It rained so hard that the truck sunk down to its frame in the mud when we got on it. We all piled off and dug it out with our bare hands while it poured cats and dogs." The children were soaked and covered with mud, and so was Leo. It was a memorable end to "a great day," and Nathan was hooked on fishing for life.

Students remember a thousand other "great days" at Weedpatch School. There was the day Edna gave Beth Stewart her first pair of earrings, and the day Beth made her first dress in sewing class for her mother. There was the day Doyle Powers got 92 percent on his arithmetic test and got to taxi the C-46 down the runway and back. There was the day when the school's first crop of potatoes came in and sold for two hundred fifty dollars. Most of the money went toward building the cafeteria, but fifty dollars was used for a trip to the Kern County Fair in Bakersfield, where over one hundred kids, Leo estimated, rode the Ferris wheel and the merry-go-round—and ate ice cream! A year later, Eddie Davis's hand-raised hog, "Eddie," placed third at the fair, but that's not what made that day special. The highlight of the day came when another boy, taller than Eddie, called Eddie a dumb Okie and Eddie stood up for himself. Eddie punched the boy in the nose and knocked him into the hog slop.

*Dress-design class with teacher
Barbara Sabovitch.*

*One of the school's cows. Eddie
Davis is the boy wearing the long-
sleeved shirt.*

Eddie was also present during what came to be known as the Fight. It was a Saturday, and most of the parents of Weedpatch Camp were working in the fields. Perhaps as many as fifty children were playing baseball at the school or swimming in the pool when three cars driven by teenage boys began to circle the playground. The teenage boys got out of the cars and squared off in front of Eddie and a line of other sixteen-year-old boys from the camp. When the intruders hurled rocks into the swimming pool, the Okie boys charged forward and the Fight was on. Some men from the camp rushed over to the playground to restore order, but by then the invaders were in retreat with bloody noses and scuffed faces. That was what the Okie children meant when they said, "It was *our school.*"

"When we started to build the school, it gave the parents hope," Leo said. "They could see what the school meant to the children. They could see it every day in their faces, in their laughter. And the

Digging an irrigation channel for the school farm.

Raising chicks for the henhouse.

longer we ran the school, the longer the families stayed. The greater portion of them stayed there and would stay the year round and work so their kids could stay in this school. They understood what we were trying to do. It was the first time the children ever had anything of their own, where all the attention was on them, where they were given the best and they knew everyone was for them." Teacher Mariel Hunter recalled a girl in the eighth grade whose family was about to move away. The girl wanted to stay in school so badly and go on to high school that she planned to marry so she could stay in town. Mariel took the problem to Leo, and Leo found the girl a home where she could live in return for doing household chores.

"Everyone pitched in to make it grow," Mariel said. "We all

worked together like one big family, and grow we did together....
The kids appreciated everything you did for them because they had
so little to light up their lives."

"The teachers made us feel important and like someone really
cared," Trice Masters said. "The school gave us pride and dignity
and honor when we didn't have those things. It was *our school*. It did
a great deal to cause us to believe we were special."

Bob Rutledge was fourteen when his family moved into the
camp. He spoke for his classmates while studying old photos of
Weedpatch School. "Look at these people," he said. "They're not
dumb." He spoke of poverty as being "in the mind" and said, "We
never accepted poverty." He described the "Okie attitude" at the
school as "This is what we are now, but it's not what we're going

*A lesson inside the C-46. The
teacher at the blackboard (wearing a
lab coat) is George Valos, who
taught math, shop, and physical
education. Betty Thompson (to the
left of Valos) taught math and
aviation mechanics. Among the
pupils are Eddie Davis (to the right,
just visible in the plaid shirt) and
Jim Montgomery (seated on the left
side, in front of Thompson).*

to be. Give us some time. Everybody should have had this experience," he added. "You have to live it to understand it."

Bob talked of a "pervading affection" between the students, the teachers, and Leo and related an example of what he meant. "The girls, when they got old enough, couldn't wear nylons because their hands were too rough from picking cotton. And they had to pick cotton to buy their dresses for the prom. But we understood," he added. "It was part of all of us, what we were and where we were going."

Surely every day was special to the four hundred or so students who attended Weedpatch School. For it was there that they learned a most important lesson: they were as good as anybody else.

NINE

Sunset School

Gradually the community around Weedpatch Camp began to hear stories about the Okie school. They heard that students were learning aircraft mechanics. They heard that the school's cafeteria served a hot breakfast for one cent and a hot lunch for two cents or offered these meals free if pupils had no money. Word spread that the teachers at the school were the best in the county and that the school had the best chemistry lab and the best equipment for learning auto mechanics. The school also became known for its lack of disciplinary problems. "We left everything laying around," Leo recalled, "and no one ever stole a thing." Members of the California Youth Authority, after visiting the school, wrote Leo commending him on "the finest crime prevention program in the State of California," but, Leo said, "There was no crime-prevention program. It was *their* school and they took pride in it."

It became clear to everyone who visited the school that the stories were true. By 1944 the once-hostile residents of Kern County were clamoring to get their children into Arvin Federal Emergency School. Amazingly, they began to phone Leo and write letters seeking to transfer their children to "the Okie school." And why not? After all, it grew its own food, raised its own livestock, had a swimming pool, a C-46 airplane, and "a richer and broader curriculum." Leo recalled, "The community that had threatened to drive the migrants out, and who resented their presence, came to accept them as part of the community when they saw what had been accomplished."

Arvin Federal *Emergency* School—the school that Okie children built from scratch—ended in 1944. The district attorney for Kern County wrote to the state attorney general in Sacramento and asked for a legal opinion about the status of the school. The legal ruling stated that an emergency could not last more than five

A view of Weedpatch School from the water tower between the school and Weedpatch Camp, showing the swimming pool and the diving board (center right) and part of the farm (lower right). The field in front of the school was used for football and other games. Part of the C-46 can be seen to the left of the school buildings.

years, and therefore Leo could no longer run his school. Accordingly, within a matter of months the school was absorbed by Vineland School District. In 1954 an earthquake destroyed all but one of the original buildings of Weedpatch School, but the school was rebuilt. Today it is known as Sunset School.

As soon as Arvin Federal Emergency School was merged into Vineland, the trustees of the district petitioned Leo for permission to let their seventh- and eighth-grade students attend the school next to Weedpatch Camp. Leo complied, and nonmigrant students enrolled by the hundreds, suddenly outnumbering the Okie children. It was no longer *their* school—but now that was of no importance. For the Okie children had learned remarkable lessons in their journey out of the Dust Bowl era—and so had the community.

And what happened to the Okie children who built the school? What became of the ragamuffins in baggy pants and tattered dresses who played with Leo in the field next to Weedpatch Camp and built their own school on the site? Willard Melton built his own desk out of orange crates and plowed the school's garden. Willard Melton is now a college professor. John Rutledge and Robert Faulkner graduated from Arvin High School as student-body presidents; John owns a mining company in Utah, Robert his own business in California. Bob Rutledge runs his own business in Bakersfield. Joyce Foster, who'd written the essay called "An Okie Man," is a high school teacher, and Jim Wren is vice principal at West High School in Bakersfield. Bill Johnson owns two supermarkets in Kern County, Tommy Ross and James Peel own construction companies in Hawaii and California, Jim Montgomery owns two restaurants in Boise, Idaho, and his brother Bruce is a

The pool. Willard Melton is second from the left, with his hand on his chest.

marketing manager for IBM. Joe Collins is a judge, while Patty Anderson and her sister, two of the school's few black pupils, became teachers in Los Angeles. Patsy Lamb graduated from college as a nutrition specialist, Doyle Powers became a mechanical engineer, and Trice Masters became a high school principal. Among the others there are legal secretaries, postal clerks, captains in the Kern County Fire Department, and a consultant investigator for the California Department of Industrial Relations.

Carlton Faulconer, who owns an insurance company in Santa Ana, California, spoke for the Okie children who built Weedpatch School: "I'm not ashamed of where I came from," Carlton said. "I'm proud of my family. I'm proud of what I did. And I'm proud of where I am today."

Writing class. Bill Johnson is in the center of the picture, wearing a T-shirt.

Weedpatch School "had a happy ending," Leo Hart said. In an old photograph of himself and five of his pupils, he is holding one of the children, and she is wearing his hat. "See that girl," he said. "Sometimes when she wasn't ready to go to school, I had to hold her and walk her around outside until she was ready. She liked to wear my hat."

Reflecting on a thousand memories of the school, Leo observed that the collection of photos is incomplete. The photos of the swimming pool don't show how much work went into building it. Seeing a picture of four hogs in a pen, Leo said, "We had over twenty hogs and we had twelve dairy cows—and we used to give milk to the kids to take back to the camp."

He remembered the faces as if taking roll call. "That's Patsy Lamb. That's Denny I told you about. And there's little Elyse Phillips and her sister Ruth. Elyse was especially good in geography. In one classroom we had a Congoleum rug on the floor with a map of the United States, and out of that the teacher developed social studies, arithmetic, reading, and geography lessons—a whole unit."

Some of Weedpatch School's first pupils. Patsy Lamb, who had cried with her family by the side of the road when they first saw the San Joaquin Valley from Tehachapi Grade, is in the center of the second row, wearing a white sweater. Paul Russell, son of camp manager Dewey Russell and a pupil at the school, is in the middle of the back row (smiling, dark crew-neck sweater). Cecil Melton, Willard's brother, is to the left in the second-from-back row, wearing a striped shirt and jacket. In front and to the right of him is Tommy Ross (dark hair). Jim Montgomery is standing in the third-from-back row, directly in front of the woman wearing the white sweater.

His eye caught a photo of Okie children standing in the field next to Weedpatch Camp. "You know," he said, "history is always full of choices. It's possible to achieve anything. Look at these kids, and look at what they've become."

Afterword

In 1944 Leo Hart was elected to a second four-year term as Kern County superintendent of education, and his innovations continued.

Leo created a mobile program to educate Okie children in the outlying areas of Kern County. The shop teacher was assigned the task of towing a trailer packed with hand and power tools, which were used to teach carpentry, mechanics, and a variety of other practical skills. A typing teacher drove a bus outfitted with typewriters mounted on the back of each seat, and a music teacher drove a truck crammed with various instruments.

Leo also started the first school for handicapped children in the county by establishing four classrooms at Kern General Hospital (now Kern Medical Center). Today the program serves more than three thousand handicapped children.

Having served two terms as superintendent, Leo accepted a position as an educational consultant to the Korean government. After two years, he returned to Kern County and served as superintendent of the Pondham Union School District until his retirement in 1959.

On November 18, 1988, Leo was present at the dedication ceremony for the newly built Leo B. Hart Elementary School in Bakersfield. He was ninety-one years old. Leo Hart died on May 30, 1989, and Edna Hart passed away two months later.

Bibliographic Note and Picture Credits

Much of the general information relating to conditions in Oklahoma, the migration, life in an Okieville, and the anti-Okie attitude in California comes from Walter Stein's *California and the Dust Bowl Migration* (Westport, Connecticut: Greenwood Press, 1973) and James Gregory's *American Exodus: The Dust Bowl Migration and Okie Culture in California* (New York: Oxford University Press, 1989).

"Sunny Cal," "Goin' Down the Road Feelin' Bad," and other Okie songs are reprinted in Charles Todd and Robert Sonkin's article "Ballads of the Okies," in *The New York Times Magazine* (November 17, 1940) and "Keep on goin' on" may be found in the *Westly Worldbeater* (May 22, 1942). "Tow-Sack Tattler" appears in Gregory, *American Exodus*, p. 145.

Concerning John Steinbeck's description of dead time in Chapter 3 ("There is no work...") and his comments on growers burning surplus crops, see John Steinbeck, *Their Blood Is Strong* (San Francisco: Simon J. Lubin Society, 1938) and David Sheff, "Fifty Years of Wrath: John Steinbeck's *The Grapes of Wrath*: 1939–1989, The People Who Lived His Story...And Are Living It Now," *California* magazine (October 1989).

With the approach of the fiftieth anniversary of *The Grapes of Wrath* in 1989 many newspapers ran full-length articles on the experiences of the Dust Bowlers, providing a wealth of firsthand information relating to conditions in the Panhandle, the journey to California, and the plight of the Okies in the San Joaquin Valley. Especially helpful were: Ronald Taylor, "California Okies Look Back on Pain of the 1930s," *The Los Angeles Times* (October 5, 1980);

Irwin Speizer, "The Grapes of Wrath Leave a Lingering Taste," *Orange County Register* (August 10, 1986); Michael Szymanski, "Okies Claimed the California Dream," Burbank-Glendale *Daily News* (October 12, 1986); Richard Hanner's five-part series "*The Grapes of Wrath* Revisited," *Stockton Record* (November 16–20, 1986); Richard Colvin, "Dust Bowl Legacy," *The Los Angeles Times Magazine* (March 26, 1989); Rick Heredia, "What *Wrath* Had Wrought," *Bakersfield Californian* (April 23, 1989); Arnold Hamilton, "*Grapes of Wrath*'s Harvest," *Dallas Morning News* (July 16, 1989); and Michael Trihey and Greg Campbell, "Dust Bowl's Migrants Recall Tough, Fun Times," *Bakersfield Californian* (October 16, 1989). The words of the Okie father in Chapter 4 ("Picture how you would feel...") are quoted in William Law, "Problems of the Migratory Student," *California Journal of Secondary Education* (March 1939).

Information relating to Leo Hart and Arvin Federal Emergency School came from personal interviews with Leo Hart in Shafter, California, on February 2, 1977, and November 28, 1984; Pete Bancroft, in San Diego on November 26, 1984; Bob Rutledge, in Bakersfield on November 29, 1984, and from correspondence with other pupils and teachers. Another useful source was Leo B. Hart, "A Report on the Development of Kern County Schools, 1939-1946" (MS., n.p., n.d.), in the library at the California State University, Bakersfield. Dust Bowl students commented on their educational experiences in Kern County in some of the fifty interviews collected and cataloged under the title "Odyssey Program," housed in the library at California State University, Bakersfield.

The story of Leo Hart and the Weedpatch School first appeared in Jerry Stanley, "The Children of the Grapes of Wrath," *American West* (March-April 1986).

◆

During the late 1930s and early 1940s, the Farm Security Administration (FSA) employed photographers to document the lives of farm workers throughout the United States. The FSA was an agency of the U.S. government set up by President Franklin Delano Roosevelt's administration to provide aid to farmers and

◆

farm laborers suffering from the effects of the Great Depression.

Among the photographs in this book, the following are the work of FSA photographers: Pages 4, 9, 11, 21, by Russell Lee, courtesy of the Library of Congress. Pages 6, 7, 8, 32 (*bottom*), by Arthur Rothstein, courtesy of the Library of Congress. Page 13 by Dorothea Lange, copyright © 1982, The Oakland Museum, The City of Oakland. Pages 16, 17, 18, 19, 23, 26, 27, 29, 30, 31, 33, 36, 37, 38, 42, by Dorothea Lange, courtesy of the Library of Congress.

The photographs of Weedpatch School, the children, and the teachers (pages 41, 46–76) are from the collection of Leo Hart and are supplied courtesy of the author. Photograph on page 61 (*center*) courtesy of Barbara Sabovitch.

Photograph on page 2 courtesy of the Department of Special Collections, Stanford University Libraries. Photograph on page 25 courtesy of the Seaver Center for Western History Research, Natural History Museum of Los Angeles County. Photograph on page 28 by Horace Bristol. Photograph on page 35 UPI/Bettmann. Photograph on page 43 from the *Bakersfield Californian* collection, courtesy of the Kern County Museum.

Acknowledgments

This book would not have been possible without the assistance of Leo Hart, Edna Hart, and Pete Bancroft; former teachers Rose Gilger, Edith Houghan, Charlene McGee, Marie Marble, Vic Meyers, and Barbara Sabovitch; and former students Pete Cattani, Eddie Davis, Carlton Faulconer, Joyce Foster, Reford Hutson, Patsy Lamb, Trice Masters, Janice Newton, Patsy Newton, Doyle Powers, Nathan Reed, Bob Rutledge, Wayne Slusser, Della Stewart, and Jim Wren. Susan Shillinglaw at the Steinbeck Center in San Jose, California, and John Walden at the Kern County Library provided valuable help with research material and photographs.

Index

Page numbers in **boldface** refer to illustrations.

About the Author

Jerry Stanley was born in Highland Park, Michigan, in 1941. When he was seventeen years old, he joined the air force and was stationed in California, where he has lived ever since. Once out of the air force, he went to college, during which time he supported himself as a rock-'n'-roll drummer on weekends. He received both his master's and Ph.D. degrees from the University of Arizona. He is now a professor of history at the California State University in Bakersfield, where he teaches courses on the American West, the American Indian, and California history. He is the author of numerous articles for both scholarly journals and popular magazines. In researching the story of Weedpatch School, Mr. Stanley conducted interviews with Superintendent Leo Hart, principal Pete Bancroft, and numerous former teachers and students.

Among Mr. Stanley's hobbies are bowling, racquetball, fishing, drumming, and writing humor. His latest hobby is driving his motor scooter to work every day. He and his wife, Dorothy, have four children and live in Bakersfield. *Children of the Dust Bowl* is his first book.